NELSON
CENGAGE Learning™

Australia • Brazil • Japan • Korea • Mexico • Singapore • Spain • United Kingdom • United States

Cars

Fast Forward
Blue Level 9

Text: Carmel Reilly
Illustrations: Luke Jurevicius
Editor: Kate McGough
Design: Vonda Pestana
Series design: James Lowe
Production controller: Emma Hayes
Photo research: Corrina Tauschke
Audio recordings: Juliet Hill, Picture Start
Spoken by: Matthew King and Abbe Holmes
Reprint: Jennifer Foo

Acknowledgements
The author and publisher would like to acknowledge permission to reproduce material from the following sources: Photographs by Advertising Archive, p8; AGE Fotostock/Bartomeu Amengual, p10/Grantpix, p13; Getty Images/Hulton Archive/Stringer, p4; istockphoto.com/Andrea Gingerich, pp 3, 11 top; Newsphotos.com, p14 bottom; Newspix.com, cover, p1/Mike Clarke, p12/Bob Finlayson, p5 bottom/Sebastian Willnow, p5 top; Photolibrary.com, p8 top/Voller Ernst, pp 7, 7 bottom/Mauritius Die Bildagentur, p11 bottom/Index Stock Imagery, p6/Photolibrary.com/Science Photo Library/TRL Ltd, p14 top; Photos.com, p9.

ISBN 978 0 17 012531 4
ISBN 978 0 17 012525 3 (set)

Cengage Learning Australia
Level 7, 80 Dorcas Street
South Melbourne, Victoria Australia 3205
Phone: 1300 790 853

Cengage Learning New Zealand
Unit 4B Rosedale Office Park
331 Rosedale Road, Albany, North Shore NZ 0632
Phone: 0800 449 725

For learning solutions, visit **cengage.com.au**

Printed in Australia by Ligare Pty Ltd
7 8 9 10 11 12 13 21 20 19 18 17

Evaluated in independent research by staff from the Department of Language, Literacy and Arts Education at the University of Melbourne.

Cars

Carmel Reilly

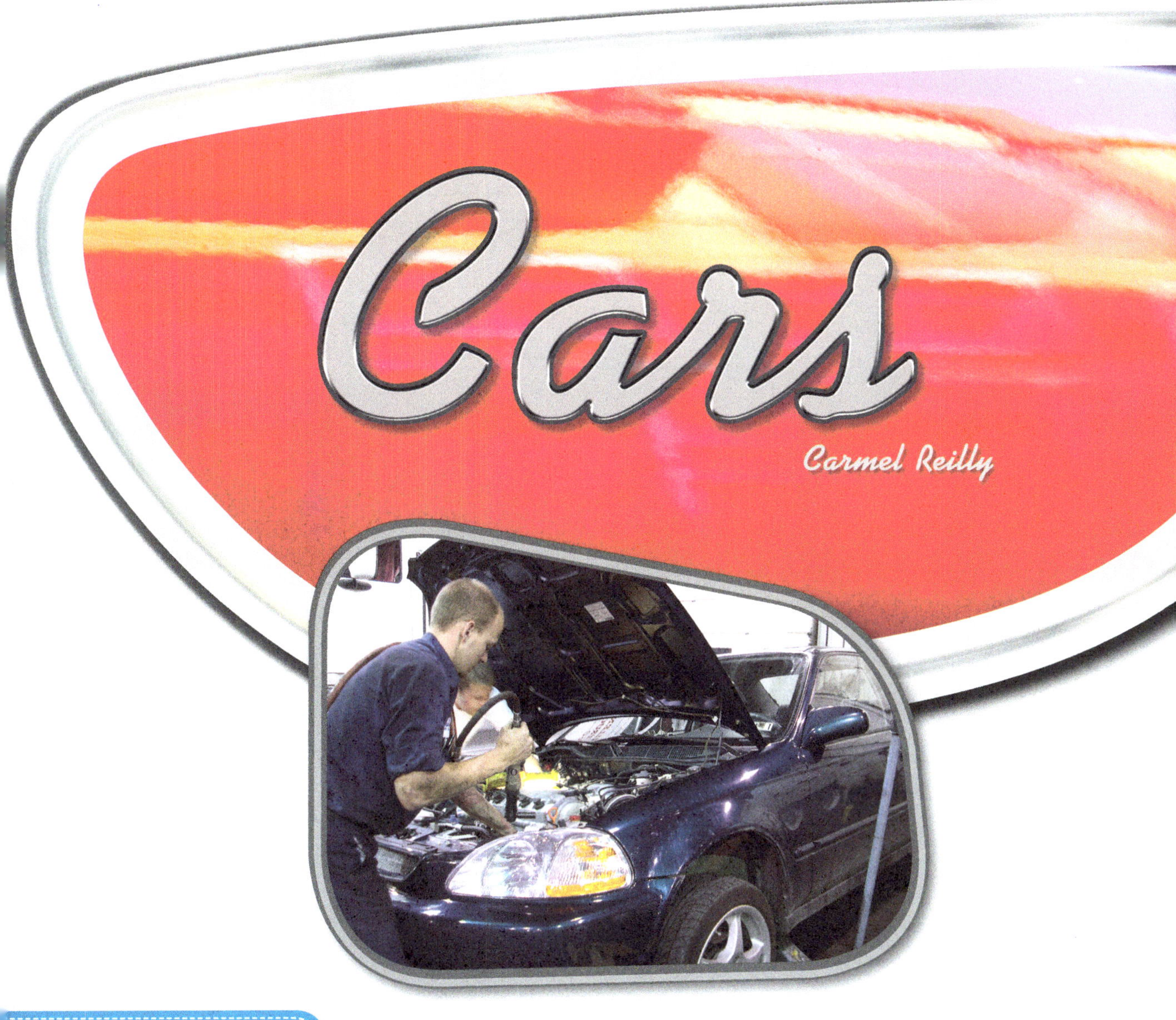

Contents

Chapter 1

THEN AND NOW

Cars were first made over 100 years ago.

In 1891, a car company in France
was the first company to make and sell cars.
They made five cars in their first year.

Today, car companies make millions of cars a year. The car industry is one of the biggest industries in the world.

Before there were cars,
trains were used to carry people and **goods**.
Trains could carry a lot of things,
but they had to go where there were railway lines.

People liked cars, buses and trucks
because they could go on any road any time.
A lot of the time,
people could drive themselves.

MORE CARS

Henry Ford

By the 1900s,
car companies had started up
all over the world.

In the USA, a car-maker called Henry Ford worked out a way to make a lot of cars quickly and sell them at low cost.

Because these cars did not cost much, a lot of people could buy them.

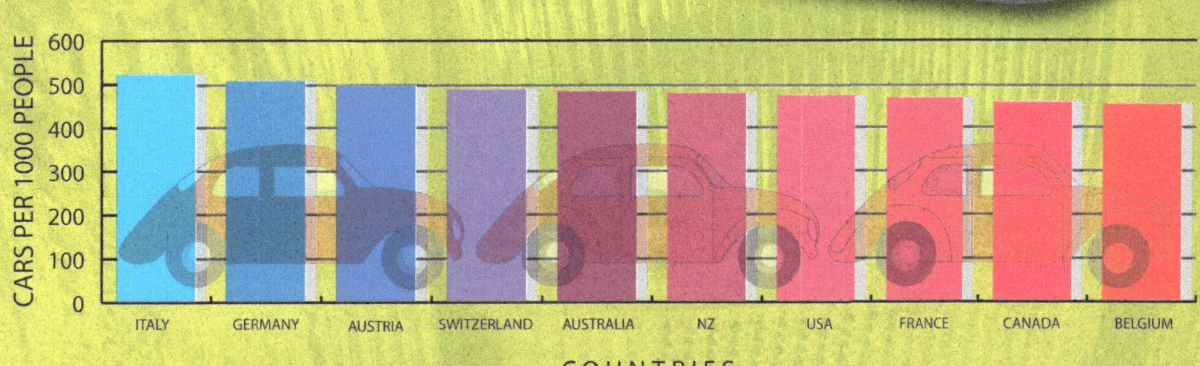

Soon, a lot of people were driving cars. Now, people in most countries have cars.

Chapter 3

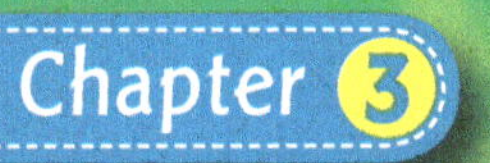

GOOD THINGS ABOUT CARS

People saw that there were good things about cars.

People could go where they wanted very quickly. Buses and trucks made carrying goods and groups of people easy.

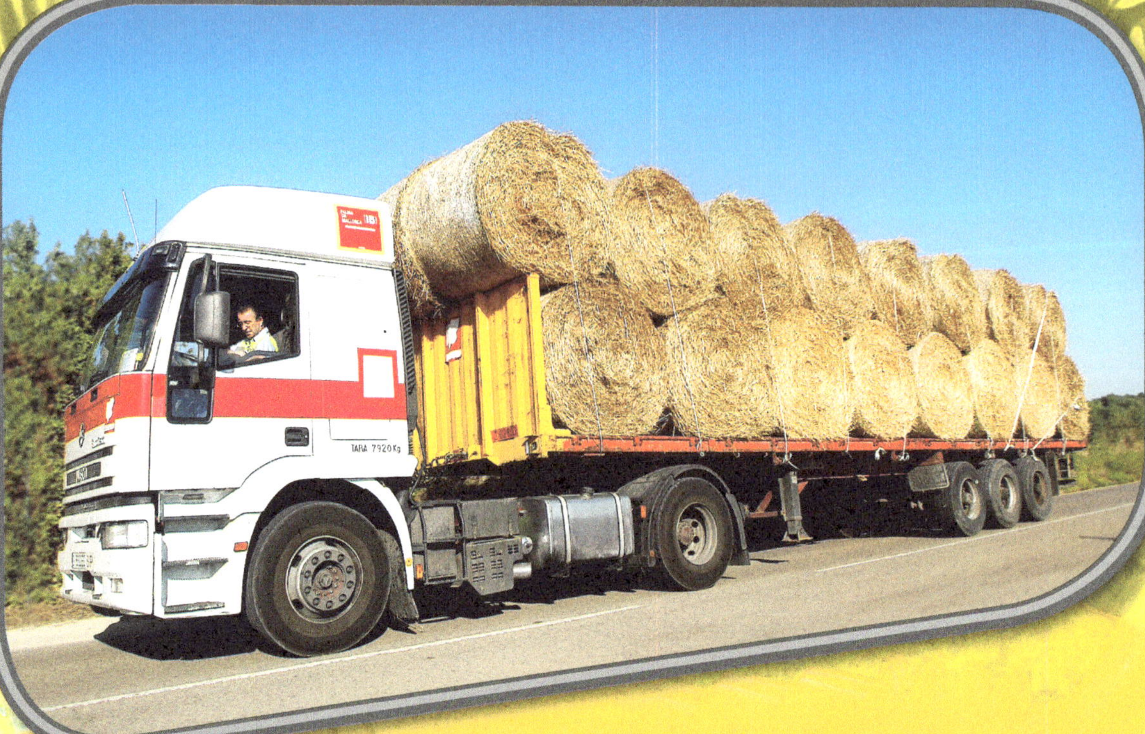

The car industry got big quickly.
A lot of people got jobs
making car parts and fixing cars.

People also got jobs making roads
for cars to drive on.
Even more people got jobs driving buses and trucks
to carry people and goods.

Chapter 4

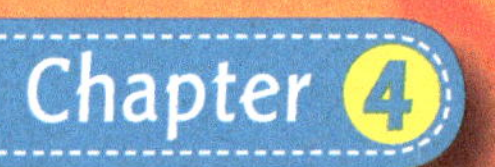

BAD THINGS ABOUT CARS

Over time, people saw that there were also bad things about cars.

Cars take up a lot of room on the roads.
It's not always easy to find a car park.
Cars also make a lot of noise,
and they make **pollution** that can hurt people
and the **environment**.

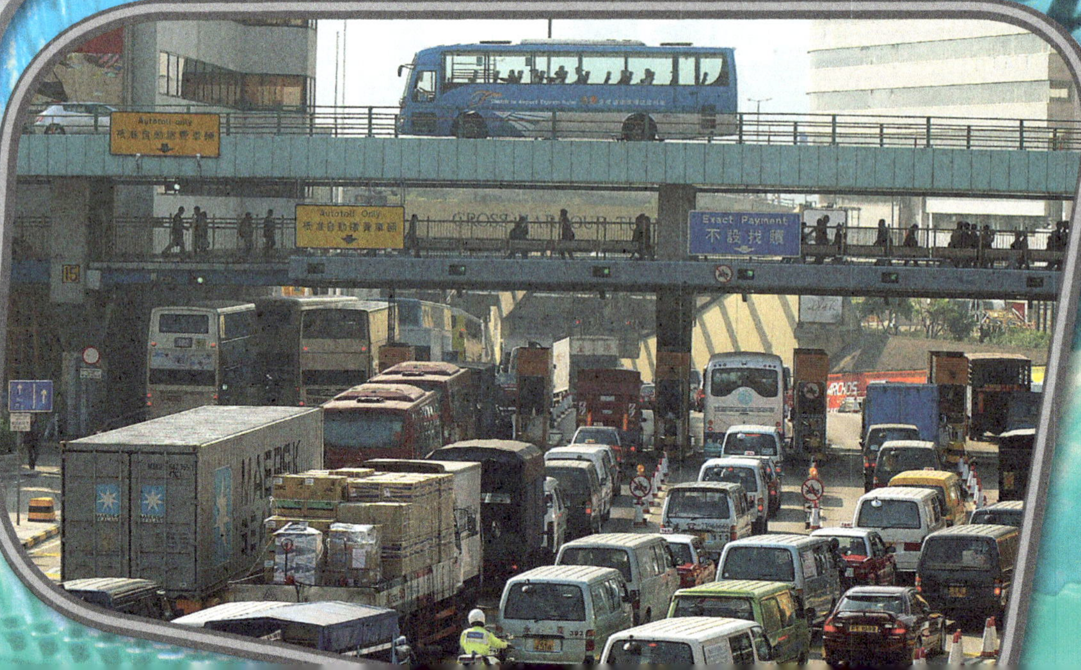

More than anything,
millions of people around the world
have been hurt or killed in car accidents
over the years.

A lot of the bad things about cars can be worked on.

A lot of car companies are making cars that are smaller, quieter and safer. They are also making cars that don't make as much pollution.

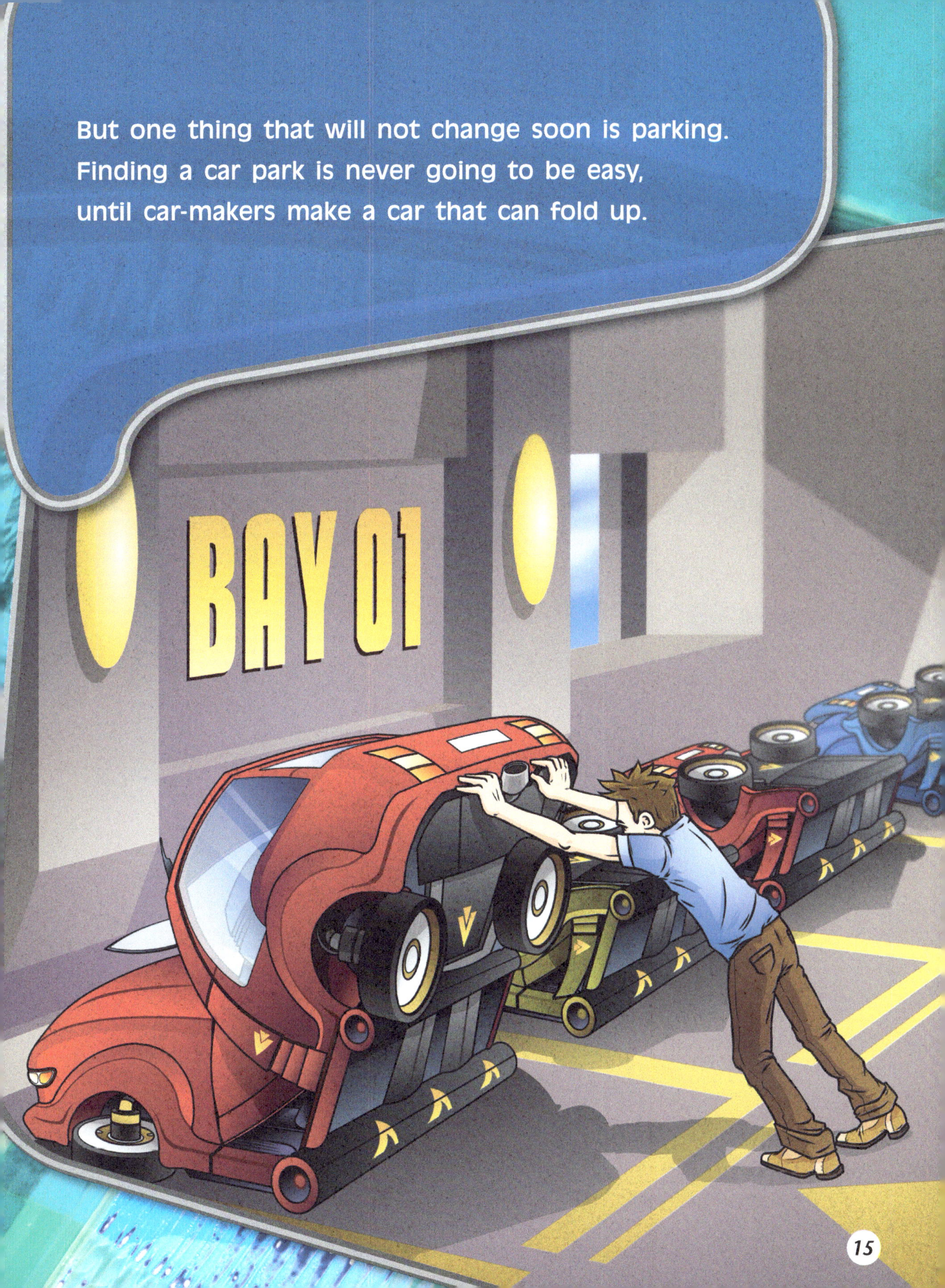

But one thing that will not change soon is parking. Finding a car park is never going to be easy, until car-makers make a car that can fold up.

Glossary

environment the world in which we live, including the earth, sea and air

goods things that we make, use, buy or sell

pollution something that can harm people and the environment

Index